In Their Boots:

Poems Inspired by Soldiers and Their Loved Ones

Book Two:
Family

G. Mark LaFrancis

Published By

M&M

Book Publishing Co.
Natchez, Mississippi
Web Site
www.inspiringauthor.org
Facebook
In Their Boots: Poems Inspired by
Soldiers and Their Loved Ones

About This Book

G. Mark LaFrancis, a veteran and an accomplished journalist and writer, has interviewed more than 100 soldiers who served in Iraq and Afghanistan and their loved ones. The interviews span more than 250 hours. They have opened their hearts and souls, offering a window into their world. Thus, a collection of poignant and enlightening poems inspired by their stories has unfolded. Some stories are funny, some uplifting, and some deeply sorrowful.

The soldiers and their families in this project have asked for anonymity, thus names have been changed, and specific circumstances altered for them.

"In Their Boots: Poems Inspired by Soldiers and Their Loved Ones" is not about the war, but about the warriors ... over there, and at home. This second volume is a tribute to the families of our soldiers. God bless them all.

HOME WITH HEROES
★ Honoring our Veterans and Loved Ones ★
A Private, Non-Profit Foundation—Facebook: Home With Heroes—Web: www.homewithheroes.org © 2013 Home With Heroes

For A Good Cause

A portion of the proceeds will be donated to the Home With Heroes Foundation Inc., a private, non-profit organization honoring and helping veterans and their loved ones.
www.homewithheroes.org
Facebook: Home With Heroes

Praise for This Work

"My U. S. Army son served two deployments, Iraq and Afghanistan, and was injured in a roadside bomb. He made it safely home and I no longer jump when the phone rings, but I often think of those who do. This incredible book of poetry reveals the heart of soldiers, their families and loved ones. Within these pages I find hope, compassion and rest."

- Richelle Putnam, author and song writer

"Reading the poems in G. Mark LaFrancis' second volume of "In Their Boots," is like hearing the voices of those whose voices are too seldom heard. LaFrancis listened to the stories of those who served in Iraq and Afghanistan. He also heard what the soldiers' families had to say. Then he wrote the poems that grace the pages of this moving, haunting, and memorable book. Iraq and Afghanistan soldiers, veterans, and their families are a silent minority. Their numbers are few - less than one percent of the U.S. population. LaFrancis' poetry gives voice to this honorable group. His writing is a celebration."

- Terrence McCarthy, author and veteran

"G. Mark LaFrancis is able to tell the stories of those who have served in a different way. I recommend that you read his poetry even if poetry is not your thing. Well done!"

- Donnie Verucchi, Past State Commander, Veterans of Foreign Wars

Dedication

This book could not have been accomplished without my own dear family and their support and love. This book is dedicated to them.

To my family
Eileen Mary Maher
My wife
Mark Maher LaFrancis
My son
Mary Maher LaFrancis
My daughter

Acknowledgments

This book could not have been accomplished without the many, many families who opened their doors, their hearts, their lives. They are truly the heroes of these armed conflicts...holding the home front, keeping watch, being strong. God bless you all. With special thanks to Army Sgt. Hunter Parker, his wife Jenna, daughter Ava and son Gus.

Table of Contents

Table of Contents

Memory Jar

Angelina wrote
A note to you
The other day
"It's a secret," she said
With "that" look
And "that" smile
"Only for Daddy.
So we made
A memory jar
For you to open
When you return
To our home
To our arms

Caleb wanted to put in
His frogs
But settled for
That Spiderman mask
You gave him
Last Halloween

And they rushed
For other things
Marbles, stickers, candies
And the little
Things of life
That are huge
In a child's eyes

As for me
Not enough
Prayers could fit

In the jar
Not enough hope
Not enough love

So I wrote a note
On simple
Lined paper
You are my love
Ever and always
This day and all the days
Of our lives

I kissed the note
Folded it
And slipped it
Among all the other stuff
In the memory jar

And so,
On the kitchen counter
Sits the memory jar.
With so much
You have given us
And your country
It is the least
We can give
You
On your
Return

Minus frogs

9

At 3 a.m.

There are no sounds
Except for the
Crickets and cicadas
At 3 a.m.
As I sit on the porch
Staring into the sky
Sometimes it is foggy
Sometimes it is clear
And there are stars
And I wonder if the
Same stars
Shine over you
There in Iraq
My son
My dear son.

There are no sounds
Except for my heavy breathing
My pounding heart
My swallowing hard
All these nights
You've been gone

I'm a strong man
A proud man
A brave man
But I'm helpless
Now
At the mercy of
Other forces
Other fears
Far beyond my
Own knowledge
And comprehension

So I sit here at 3 a.m.
On the porch
Where we last hugged
Where we last embraced
Trying to stretch my
Emotions so far
Over the stars
You might feel
My love

Packing List

Mom rolled my socks
Folded my T-shirts
And cleaned
My uniforms
"I'm missing something,"
She said, wiping away a tear.

My mom,
So thorough
So organized
So strong

Sun block
You'll need your sun block
You know how you burn
And insect repellent
I've heard the bugs are terrible.

And I watched
As Mom ran down her
Packing list
Socks, T-shirts, handkerchiefs,
Underwear,

And I checked off mine
Pictures ... sweet memories
For a soldier to carry to war.

And she turned to me
After the packing was done
I've forgotten something,
She said
What is it; I've forgotten
something

I grabbed Mom's hands
And looked into her eyes
Not as a boy, but as a man
And said,

You haven't forgotten a thing
All my years
You've been strong
You've been brave
The best single mom ever

I pulled Mom close
And felt her love
Not as a boy, but as her son
And we said nothing
And time stopped
And bowed in reverence
To a soldier and
His mom

Pancakes

Oh, yeah
Those pancakes
She made them
With a sprinkle of
Cinnamon
And sugar

A smile
A heart
Well, no, they
Weren't perfect

But man
So good

Butter
Honey
Syrup

A kiss
On my forehead

"Like 'em?"

Oh, boy,
Do I?

Damn
I'm getting
Teary-eyed
Talkin' about

Just pancakes
As night
Settles
After a long
And difficult
Day on patrol
And the bitter wind
Whips by our small platoon

I know I'm a simple guy
In a complex world
In a complex war

There's something
Soothing
Powerful
Wonderful
At looking back
When I was ten
At an innocent time
Of pancakes
Butter
Honey
Syrup
A kiss
On my forehead

By Mom
The one
The only
Pancake Queen

'Cuda

God's blessing
Laid in my arms
A newborn boy
As I hummed
"How Great Thou Art"
Little 'Cuda I nicknamed him
I really don't know why
But 'Cuda sounded cuter
Than Henry
So I called him 'Cuda

He slipped in slyly
That day in May
A clutch of flowers
Behind his back
A boy of nine
Happy Momma's Day
He yelled.
And I prayed and hummed
"How Great Thou Art"

And 'Cuda sat in front of
The congregation
And professed Jesus
As his friend and savior
A boy/man of thirteen
And I sang so proudly
"How Great Thou Art"
Indeed "How Great
Thou Art"

And 'Cuda slipped
Behind the wheel
A young man of sixteen
I closed my eyes
As he drove us to the Piggly Wiggly
Only after we arrived safely
Did I proclaim

"How Great Thou Art"

But when 'Cuda
Said goodbye
On his way to the Army
On his way to war
I clutched my heart
And almost lost my faith
But found the courage
To hum
"How Great Thou Art"

And the days passed,
He sent sweet letters
And he married
A beautiful young lady
And became a handsome man
A proud soldier
My 'Cuda
And I hummed
"How Great Thou Art"
Then, only faith became
The thread
Linking 'Cuda and me

But when boots shuffled outside
My door that night
And the bell rang
I crumpled; I folded;
I cried; I wailed
My 'Cuda
My 'Cuda
Was gone
War took him
Oh so violently
My 'Cuda
That boy who nestled
At my breast

As I hummed
"How Great Thou Art"
Was gone

But he isn't
I won't let him
'Cuda's sweet voice
Still whispers to me
'Cuda's sweet smile
Still lifts my heart
'Cuda's love
Still embraces me
And hums to me

"How Great Thou Art"

And so it is in
The remembering
The cherishing
That life with 'Cuda
Remains as beautiful
As blessed
As the day
He was born
When I hummed
"How Great Thou Art"
"How Great Thou Art"

Lion King

I know you are twenty now
Broad-shouldered
Six feet, one and a half
Trained and ready
More than a man
A Marine

The other day
While cleaning your room
I find this old tape
Of "The Lion King"
The box was worn
The tape was loose

My heart leapt back
To those days
When you sat at my right side
Our bowl of popcorn
And cups of orange Kool Aid
Watching "The Lion King"

Watching Musfasa
Watching
Cheering
At the happy ending

No matter how many times
We watched, you cringed

When the little lion was near peril
And you snuggled closer

Now there you are
Somewhere in Afghanistan
I'm not supposed to know
In real peril
Without your dad
To snuggle close,
To cheer with
At the happy ending
For we don't know the ending
For you, my son

It is why I go to sleep at night
With a heavy heart
And sometimes tears

This night, though,
I slid the tape into the VCR
And watched from beginning to end
The Lion King
And felt you
Snuggling
Into my right side
As I cried tears
Of remembrance
Tears of fear

15

Candles

Jennifer ran to her room
I know she cried
Hard
Very hard
The day you left
Your little girl
Your angel

At only eleven
She understands
So little, but feels
So much

She came out
A candle in her hand
Her smile beaming
And she proudly pronounced

I know what we'll do
Every night we'll light
A candle
When Daddy's gone
Every night

I smiled and drew
Her to me

Hugged her
And said
Angel, that might be
A lot - a lot - of candles

She looked at me
As if to say
And ...

So, the next day
We bought boxes
And boxes of candles
Hoping that
In the lighting
Of them
You feel our love
As Angel said,
When Daddy looks up
He'll see the stars
And our candles

And I said softly
He'll also feel the warmth
Of our love

Casserole

I carried the casserole,
My wife's best
Tuna casserole,
To the house
Two doors down
To the house
With the U.S. flag
Flying
To the house
Where soldiers
In full dress
Just two nights before
Arrived
With "that" news
About Jeremy
Who mowed our lawn
Who babysat our kids
Who came to my door
The day my husband died
After a struggle with cancer
And, tears in his eyes,
Brought a casserole
From his mom

The same Jeremy
Who returned from Basic
A taut, proud young man
Who "friended" me on Facebook

Oh, Jeremy
You were like
The son I never had
The son I wish
For everyone
As I carry the tuna casserole
My husband's specialty
Your favorite
To your Mom and Dad
And family
As they
As we
Mourn

The loss
Of one of the
Best damn
Young men
God ever
Placed on Earth

I stood
Outside your door
Casserole
In hand
As my
Heart
Crumbled

Christmas Lights

"Damn!"
I hollered, shaking the lights
Those spaghetti strands
Of wire-thin webs
That refused to separate
As I sat on the front lawn
Angry and frustrated
Because…well, because
Unlike Dad
I couldn't do this

And Mom yelled out the front door
"Son, don't cuss; they're only
lights."

"Ha!" Only lights
They're Christmas lights
The lights Dad put up
Perfectly
Since I was, what, six?
And Mom wanted to take a photo
And send it to him
Over in Afghanistan
To show him that we were keeping
His Christmas lights alive
And bright
And shining

My temper was hot
My hands were cold

But I shook the lights
Untwisted them
And managed to line the roof
And even spread some on the
bushes

Mom got the camera
I plugged the lights in
And wow, most even worked
"Quick, shoot, before they blow
out!"

And so on its way
Is a photo
Of me, mouth wide open
Below the crooked strand
Of Christmas lights
Some working
Some not

And Dad,
We left the others
In the box
Waiting for
More skillful hands
To untwist and untangle
And bring them to life
And warm our hearts
Again

Show and Tell

Jessica had just presented
Her father
A fireman

He showed us
His Air Pac
His suit
His boots
His axe
Or "chopper"
As Jessica
Called it
Applause
Oooh
Ahhh
For
Jessica's
Dad.
Even I
Was impressed

And Adam's dad
A cartoonist
Drew funny people
Before our
Very eyes

Jan's mom
A singer.
Applause
Even mine

Then,
It was my turn
For
Show and tell

I slid slowly
From my seat
To the front of
The room
And looked at
Mrs. Colbert
She nodded back

And there on the screen
Behind me
Was my dad
A Marine
A soldier
In Iraq
"Hey, kids," he said
Smiling
In his uniform
I beamed
My dad
Was there
For Show and Tell
For me
Across thousands
Of miles

And they sat
In a trance
As my Dad
Spoke

"Hey, kids
Hope y'all are having
A good time
At Show and Tell."

"Over here in Iraq

It's really hot
This is my bunk;
Not very fancy
And my pack
Here's my rifle"

There were oohs

"Over here is the wall
Where we put up all
The cards and drawings
You sent
We love 'em
Please send more"

They all were
Riveted to his words
To his voice
As was I

"You may hear and see a lot
You may not like the war
You may wish bad things
Didn't happen."

"But we are here

Protecting you
We are here
Caring for you
So only good things
Happen to you"

The signal slipped away
Into grayness
We sat
At our desks
Left to us
To absorb
To feel
To know
What the men
And women
Live through
Over there
Far from
Us
Far from
Home
Far from
Show and
Tell

Mud Pies

Now, Mommy
Squeeze it tight
Our daughter, Angel
Said that morning
When we made
The most
Wonderful mud pies

She instructed me
To get out the moisture
Just as you had done
And she reminded me
This is how Daddy said
To do it

And I squeezed
And squeezed
Good, Mommy
We spread the pie batter
And slid the pie into the
Fake oven
She set the timer
For three minutes
Now we talk
She said
Daddy and I talk

You miss Daddy
I asked
Wrong question

No, Mommy
She said
You need to ask me
If we'll need whipped cream
If we'll have enough.
I sat puzzled
Okay, I said

Will we have enough
Whipped cream

And she laughed
No one wants
Whipped cream on a
Mud pie
She laughed and laughed
And I laughed, too

But will we have enough
I asked
And she laughed again
We'll have plenty
Daddy always said that
She laughed again
We'll have plenty because ...?

She looked at me as if
Begging and answer
Well, I'm not sure, Angel

She laughed and said
Because no one wants
To really eat mud pies!

She fell over laughing
And I did too
We laughed and laughed
Almost until we cried

I hugged her tight
And felt you in my arms too
With Angel
And mud pies
And laughter
And tears

Sponge Bob

The box arrived
Just in time
Just before
We set out
To meet with
Local Afghan leaders
And talk
And listen
And understand
And try to bridge
Gaps, wide gaps

And your box
With goodies
Arrived
We stuffed our
Pockets
And our faces, too

There on the top
Was Angel's
Sponge Bob
His smile
Reminded me
Of yours
My sweet
Goofy
Little
Girl

Home now
And now I sit
On the bedroom floor
Unpacking
Boots
Uniforms
And stuff

And you walk in
Damn how I missed
Your dimples
Your brilliant eyes
Your ever-so-sweet smile

And I remember
Sponge Bob
Your friend
You sent to me

You looked around
I knew

I brought you close to me
And said
Angel, Daddy went
To a place where
People sometimes didn't
Have homes
Or candy
And children
Didn't even have pencils
Or any Sponge Bobs

My dear Angel
I said to her
I gave your Sponge Bob
To a little girl
Who didn't even
Have shoes

And tears
Dripped down
My cheeks

Remembering that girl

And fearing my girl
Would think
I gave her dear friend away
Instead
Angel hugged me tight
And said
Oh, Daddy
It's all right

I'm a big girl now
I melted
From her wisdom
Her understanding
And I realized
Angel didn't send me
Sponge Bob
But herself

Memorial Day

We went to the cemetery
That morning
Memorial Day
I'm a Senior Patrol Leader
For Scout Troop 168

My dad was a veteran
His father, too;
So was my grandfather,
And his father and his father's father

The wind whipped our flags
As my buddies and I
Found veterans' graves
And planted the flags

We came to one grave
A fresh one
It was Jimmy's uncle Gregory
He died in Afghanistan

About a month ago
And Jimmy knelt
And put his flag
In the soft soil

We gave a Scout salute
And I felt something
Important was happening
For Jimmy
For me
For my father
For my grandfather

The wind whipped our flags
As my buddies and I
Found veterans' graves
And planted the flags
That Memorial Day

His Chair

It is blue
His chair
His favorite color
His favorite spot
To watch the news
Law and Order
Basketball
Bowling

His chair
We have kept
So clean
So fresh
Just for him

Where he ate pizza
Where he read
The newspaper
Where he laughed
Where he cried

But now
What are we to do
With his chair
What are we to do
With our sadness.

He's gone

Consumed by war
We can't understand
He's gone
Yet his chair
Remains
I remember so well
That night
That terrible night
They came to our door
I slumped into his chair
Hoping it would hug me
With his strength
Only coldness enveloped me
And left me hurt,
Saddened, stripped
Of feelings

So I sat in his chair
Letting him
Into my soul
Once more
Hoping he
Left behind
In his chair
Enough of
His strength
For me

Man of the House

He took me aside
My dad did
The night before he left
His strong hand
On my small shoulder
All those years of being his son
Feeling his hand lifting me
Making me strong

You're the man of the house
Now, son
He said
Squeezing firmly, but gently
I don't know if I'll be back
I sure pray to God I will
But while I'm away
Be as good as you've ever been
Be as strong as I would have been

Your mom may cry
Not about you
Your sisters may fuss
Not about you
But about those things
They cannot control
They cannot see
They cannot feel
And you my son
May do the same

But each day
At sunrise and sunset
I'll say a prayer
A special prayer
For you

I hugged Dad hard
I'll pray for you, too, Dad

They're here,
Mom hollered to Dad
We broke our hug
He grabbed his duffel bag
I followed him to the front door
Hugs and kisses
Squeezes and tears
Swallows
Hard swallows

Dad bounded down the walk
To the blue military bus
He looked back at me
His eyes so clear
So strong
He winked
I winked back
Through tears

At sixteen
I've acted
As though
I've known it all
At sixteen
I've pretended
I'm a man

But now
There is no acting
No pretending
I've got to be
The man
My Dad wants
Me to be
I've got to be
The man
I've learned
My Dad is

Boots on Boards

Boots on boards
Fingers on bells
Screen doors squeak.
Ma'am, we regret
To inform you . . .
Your beloved . . .
Fought bravely . . .
A credit to his country . . .
You should be proud . . .
Oh, Henry, our Jeff
Our Jeff . . .
Are you sure?
Are you sure?
A fine young man
Credit to
His country
Be proud
Be proud

Oh, I'm forgetting
My manners.
Some tea?

Biscuits?
No, Ma'am
Are you sure?
Yes Ma'am
We're sure

Our Jeff?
So young,
Here's his picture
Yes, Ma'am
A fine-looking ...

Didn't even
Say goodbye
Barely shaved
Are you sure?
Yes, Ma'am

Didn't even
Say goodbye ...

Eagle Badge

Dan Jr.
Wished for this moment
Since he was eleven
To earn his Eagle Badge
Scouting's highest honor
Oh, so different now
Than he was
As a Tiger Cub
In effervescent orange
Non-stop "kidness"
And on into Cubs
And knots
And salutes
And learning
About citizenship
And how to fold the flag
The one I saluted every time
I went on drill weekends
In my uniform

As a Boy Scout
He earned pins and badges
Rose in the ranks
He learned to cook
And bandage
And to call me Sir
And his mom, Ma'am
And to recite that law
"A Scout is Trustworthy,
Loyal, Helpful, Friendly,
Courteous, Kind, Obedient,
Cheerful, Thrifty, Brave,
Clean, Reverent"

As I listened to words
From his fellow Scouts
And his Scoutmaster

About his kindness
His leadership
His bravery
Tears came to
My eyes
That's my son
I thought
I didn't give him
Enough credit
Enough respect

He rose
To receive his badge
The Eagle Scout badge
The highest honor
A Scout can achieve

He came to me
Whispered in my ear
Thanks, Dad
And wheeled me to the
Center of the floor
His Scoutmaster
Slipped into my palm
The Eagle Badge
Dan Jr. bent down
And I worked the pin
Into his shirt
My hands weren't
Very steady yet
In fact
Nothing about me
Was very steady

He hugged me tight
Son, I said,
I'm so proud

So proud

Soldier
And Scout
Father
And Son
And there we were
Each embracing
Each in the other's
Heart
The perfect moment
That day
When my son

Received his
Eagle Badge
He's a pilot now
Flying high
Like that Eagle
He calls once in a while
Says he's all right
Say's he's an Eagle

And my heart pounds
With utter pride

For my Eagle

Old Fatigues

Billy and I looked through the shed
The other day
And found your duffel bag
Filled with your old fatigues
Remember those stiffly starched
Green things?
They weren't as stiff
As you remembered
Or wanted
And we found your old boots
Your old insignias
Your old socks

And Billy put on the cap
You wore the day

You graduated from
Combat School
And Billy saluted me and smiled

And I remembered
How you looked
So handsome in
Those
Old fatigues

And that day
I hugged your shirt
As if
You were still
In it

Dog Tags

They rattle
Around my neck
My copy of
Your Dog Tags
Name
Rank
Serial Number

Oh, Dear Jerry
The clanking
The rattling
Is music
To me
Like a symphony
Of love
And hope

Oh, Dear Jerry
Sometimes
When no one sees
I kiss the Dog Tags
And hold them
To my chest
And say a prayer
For your safety
My strong soldier
Trying to do your duty
Trying to be strong
Somewhere
In Afghanistan

And Jerry
Each night
I hold tight
These thin
Strips of metal
And pray
And say
Oh my love
Be safe
From harm
Return home
To our arms
But in the night
When the kids
Are blessed with sleep
I cannot embrace
The solace of slumber
So I sit in my chair
Next to yours
In our den
And reach out
To where your hand
Used to be
And pretend
You are with me
As I clutch
Your Dog Tags

And my heart pounds
Deep into the night

New Tie

We bought Timmy
A nice clip-on
Royal blue
Tie
He just turned ten
I just turned thirty
I never knew how
To tie a real tie

He lost his Daddy
I lost my Tim
And there we were
Worrying about
His tie

The day
We were to say
Farewell to my Tim
And his Daddy
The day
Tim wanted to wear
His Dad's tie
Not a clip-on
But a real tie
His Dad's tie

So I draped
Timmy's tie
Around his son's neck
And tightened it
And looked into
Timmy's eyes
And he looked
Into mine
And tears flowed
On this

The hardest day
Of our lives

You
Look
So good
I whispered
In Timmy's ear
And hugged
Him so tight

He whispered
I feel so bad

Me, too
Me, too

But he sat
So proud
As my heart
Almost
Collapsed
As the soldier
Presented him
With the Flag

He straightened
His tie
And embraced
His father's Flag
As tears flowed
Down his face
And fell
On his
New tie

Scrapbook

Your simple brown paper box
Arrived today
But inside
Jewels glistened
In the scrapbook
Of our lives
Together

Us with the dolphins
Off Florida's coast
Us with Mickey and Minnie
At Disney World
Us cooking spaghetti
In our first kitchen
For our first
Family meal

The guys
Wanted a look
No way
These are
My jewels
Our jewels
In that simple brown paper box

Us with Molly
The mutt we rescued
From the pound
Us with that
Ecstatic, giddy, exhausted
Look when Tim arrived
Made two into three

And then four
With Amy
More reasons
To savor life

In that simple brown paper box
You brought us
To life for me
In this
A place
Where life
May end
At any moment

Until
That simple brown paper box
Arrived
There were no jewels
Just days of duty
Of wariness
Of weariness
Of soldiers

Now I have
Gems
Aplenty
And my love
For you
Has grown
Only deeper
A gem amid chaos
A jewel amid destruction

Jimmer

Jimmer
Laid his weary
Head on my lap
Tonight

Jimmer
Hugged the picture
Of you
Tonight

Jimmer
Asked why his mommy
Was crying
Tonight

Jimmer
Drew of picture
For his daddy
Tonight

Jimmer
Told his sister
His daddy's a hero
Tonight

You're the Best

In all of this
I have learned
A lesson, My Dear,
That has transformed
Who I am
And how I think

I have discovered
The simple truth:
You're the best

It took me
The separation of
Three thousand miles
To realize what
I should have known
All along:
You're the best

It took me to see
The worst
In humanity
To see
You're the best

It took me the
Most intense longing
To be back home
To you to realize
You're the best

It took me far
Too long to realize
You're the best.

Don't Forget Me

She looked me in the eyes
She touched my cheeks
And sighed
Don't forget me
Please

Not a command
But an appeal
On this the day
I hugged her tight
And whispered
My love
Into her ear

And grabbed my duffel
And strode to the bus
With the other striding troops

I stopped

Turned
Blew a kiss
And mouthed
Don't forget me

Our eyes
Lingering
The longest time
Our hearts
Breaking
Our souls
Reaching
To embrace
One another

Don't forget me
I mouthed the words
Don't forget me

At 10:18

Carlee broke her crayon
Again
And Julius looked sleepy
Again
And Jewel colored so perfectly
Again

At 10:18

Sam needed to go to the bathroom
Again
My desk looked like a mess
Again
Velee cried
Again

At 10:18

And so, too, did I cry
No, not openly
No, not so my pupils could see
Or hear

At 10:18

That minute is burned
In my mind
In my memory
In my heart
Forever

My Dan
My strong Dan
My Marine Dan
Died
At 10:18
So the report said
Of Dan's passing

In that firefight
That claimed
Six Marines

So that moment
So precise
Is etched
In my mind
In my heart
For all time

So at 10:18
I got Carlee another crayon
Woke up Julius
Smiled at Jewel
Gave Sam a bathroom pass
Ignored my desk
Comforted Velee
Whose grandmother
Died the week before

I stop
Each day
At 10:18
And force back tears

For my children
Need me, too.
Just, dear husband,
As I needed you

But I can't have you
Not in my arms
But in my heart
In my memory
As the best man
God ever made

The Red Dress

Abby
My sweet
Girl of nine
Innocence
Sweetness
A child
Of wonder
And hope

Sent dresses
To me

"Give these
To the children
Of Iraq
Daddy
And please
Find a special
Girl for
My red dress"

There were dresses
Bows, socks, toys,
Stuffed animals
Shoes, tops, shorts
And so much love
In the box

I could smell her lilac
Essence
Damn, Sarge said
Sweet kid
Sweet kid

At that moment
I wanted to rush
To the streets
Sharing my girl's gift
With whomever
I met

But I knew
A red dress
Worn proudly by
A child there
Would be seen as
A target here
And so I slipped
Abby's gift
Into my room
As a reminder
Of the beauty
I left behind
Of the beauty
That awaits me

Muscles

"Daddy,"
Angel hollered
"Do, it, Daddy!
Puhleese."

So I did
As my Angel
Commanded

Been to Iraq
And Afghanistan
Twice
And no lieutenant
Could make me jump
Like my Angel

So I stood tall
In the back yard
As the burgers sizzled
On the barbecue
And my bride fixed
Potato salad
I rolled up my sleeve
Like I did
Before
Well, you know

And I curled my arms
Letting my muscles pop
I called with a crisp
"Ten-Hut"
As my biceps
Stood at attention

Before my tours
Angel would squeal
With glee
And hang on my arm

As we laughed and laughed
But this time
As I beamed at her
She frowned
"Dad," Angel said,
Pointing to the hose
"I mean like
Fill the pool."

So I grabbed the hose
And began to fill the pool
Thinking the months
The years over there
I had lost the years
Over here

As the water gurgled
And my mind drifted
To places
To people
To things
I feared
I might never
Be home

Until Angel
Snapped my attention
She grinned
A huge grin
She had her arm
Showing her bicep
And proclaimed
"I've got my own muscles
Now, Daddy."

Sometimes
I have to be reminded
I am really home

39

Just Hold Me

How can I tell you
How a wife lives
While her man is away
Away to war

How can I tell you
About sitting on the couch
After a day
The bills came in
The dishwasher clogged
The car broke down
And Angel laid in my arms
Sick with fever
And we missed Jimmy's game
And...
And...

And I sit there
Staring at his picture

And thinking
Praying
Hoping
Needing
Wanting
Crying
Just hold me, dear
Come home
Just hold me

Just
Hold
Me

Jacob's Book

It came to me one day
To do a book for Jacob
Of all those years
He spent as a boy
And a young man
So when he returned
He'd see it and be proud
And be happy
That his mom would
Do this for him

So I got a nice scrapbook
At the stationery store
A bit costly
But oh, well, it's for Jacob
And I dragged out the boxes
And boxes of memorabilia
Oh, so many photographs
He did so much
As a boy Scout
A Bobcat in orange
A Cub in blue
A Scout in tan
Mud fights with Jim
His next-door buddy
The science fair
His rocket so tall
The basketball game
When he scored eight
And Christmases
And the simple
And silly times
When he trained the puppy
To lick him on command
And the time he climbed
On the roof
And the time he took

His sister trick-or-treating
On his own

Boxes of photographs
The prom
High school graduation
His first car
His first girlfriend
His first computer
He loved so much
Days into years
All compressed
Into one book
Jacob's Book
With his picture
On the outside
The one of him
I took
When he was ten
And had a missing tooth
Just before he said
Love ya Mom

And I hugged
Jacob's Book
To my breast
That autumn morning
Wind whistling through
The trees and pushing my hair
As I heard Taps
Played off in the distance
As my fallen soldier
Was laid to rest
At the National Cemetery
And tears fell
From my eyes
Onto Jacob's Book

The Show

We left the picture show
Anna, Caleb and me
We saw
Shrek 3
We laughed and laughed
Like you did
On our couch
With Shrek 1 and Shrek 2
When Caleb
Laughed so hard
He got the hiccups
And popcorn
Got knocked
To the floor
And Molly lapped it up
And I laughed so hard
I cried
And I wished
That moment
Would last forever
Beyond us
And into our
Hearts and souls

But forever
Had to wait
The war called you
And you left
Not laughing
But weeping
I know you did
Even though you held

Back tears
As I did

And now we wait
For your return
Anna and Caleb
Still watch Shrek
And giggle
And spill popcorn

And Caleb insists
We leave a space
On the couch
For you
As if you are here
Laughing
And
Hiccuping
And spilling
Popcorn
That Molly
Eats
At our feet

And I leave
A space in
My heart

That only
You
Can
Fill

42

Dear Soldier

Dear Soldier
Our teacher told us to write to you
We'd get extra credit
I kinda need the extra credit
So I did

Dear Soldier
Do you like shoot people?
I hope not
I understand tho'
If their the enemy
Kinda like want to shoot you

Dear Soldier
I only read about war
Not about your war
But the old wars
World War 2, Vietnam
Wars like that

My teacher said

Soldiers are all alike
No matter what the war
No matter what the mission
No matter what color
No matter what gender
No matter what age
She said soldiers are
Wonderful people
Who risk their lives for us
For me

Dear Soldier
I'm just a kid
But I care
I don't know you
But I care
Please come home
Dear Soldier
Whether I get extra credit
Or not

Fried Chicken

We used to sit at the dinner table
My brother Aaron and me
And challenge each other
To eat the most of
Grandma's fried chicken
And Grandma would
Laugh and laugh
I always won
I'm a big boy of two-fifty
Nose tackle for the Bears
Stocker at the Wal-Mart

And Aaron, well
He went into the Marines
He always was sharp
Kept his room neat and organized
Changed the oil in his car
Mowed and trimmed the lawn

The day Aaron left
The darkest day of my life
The day this big guy cried
The day I wanted to
Crawl into a dark hole
But I didn't

Grandma and I watched the news
Almost all the time
CNN was on our TV
We heard from Aaron
He got promoted not once,
But twice
He said pray for him
And we did
At supper ... fried chicken
We held hands

Blessed the food
And prayed that the Lord
Would keep Aaron safe

Grandma called me at Wal-Mart
That night ... that terrible night
When we got the word
An explosion ... a firefight

That night the soldiers came
And we learned
Aaron was dead
So far away

Grandma busied herself
Trying to cook
Trying to be Grandma

But for me
I was never nothing
But Aaron's brother
His buddy

My heart
Cried so hard
That night
I just knew
It was going
To explode

Grandma and I hugged
And we cried
For hours
And hours
Deep into the next day

People came by
With casseroles
And tears
And sat for a while
My boss at Wal-Mart
Brought food - lots of it
And patted me on the back
Son, we'll take care of you
He said

As I wept in my thanks

I didn't want food
Or pats
Or anything
But Aaron
Sitting next to me
With a big platter
Of Grandma's fried chicken

Moving

Gayle's pink guitar
Sam's gerbils
My jewelry box
That he made
From his hands
From his tools
That we sold at the
Tag sale last week
Were there
Ready for moving
From the base
That has been our home
To wherever our
New home might be:
My Mom's
His Parents'

We have not yet finished
Our tears
Our goodbyes
And we're moving
Gayle's pink guitar
Sam's gerbils
My jewelry box

The crackle of the
Twenty-one gun salute
Filled my ears

The soulful Taps
Reverberated
In my heart
As Sam and Gayle
Clutched my hands
While wiping tears
The folded flag in my arms

Neighbors
Wives mostly
Whose husbands
Still have their lives
Over there
Come and hug and offer
Best wishes
And cry

Knowing they too
Could be moving

We are military wives
You don't hear much about

We live on the edge
We live on the hope
We'll embrace our men again
And not their coffins

Bedside

We knew he was dying
We hated to know
But we knew
We knew he knew, too

Ralph lay in the hospital bed
Tubes flowed from him
Tubes flowed to him
Disease consumed him

Who knows how?
Agent Orange
Defoliants?
Just life?

My proud
My strong
My loving
Man

Lay
Drifting
From me

Damn

He was the proudest
Marine on the planet
Raised by a Marine
Who was raised by
A Marine
You get the picture

He lived

And loved
Semper Fi
Hoo Ha

And I loved
Him for that

And I gripped my
Marine's strong hand
Not wanting to let go
Not wanting to surrender
No real Marine ever surrenders

The hospital room door opened
And in stepped you my son
Our son
Whisked from the parade
grounds
At Camp Lejeune
Whisked here to your dad's side
Whisked in your beautiful
uniform
To your father's bedside

When I looked at you
I realized
My man in the bed
Wasn't fading away
But being relived
In you

Your strong hand
Gripped my soft shaky hand

"I made it, Mom.
"I made it."

And you leaned over
To your dad
"I made it, Pop;
"I made it;
"I'm a Marine."

And I sat through the night
With my Marine men
One falling behind
One moving ahead
By morning
We lost one
And gained another

Be Like This

It was never supposed to
Be like this
For God's sake
I'm a Christian
A good man
A good father

Yet I'm a prisoner
In a jail cell
Whose key
I cannot find

My son
The Marine
The young man
Who ran touchdowns
Who fought off the ladies
Who made me proud

Now sits in his room
Crippled by his past
Enveloped by his present
A room of contradictions
Of what was
And what is

I enter his world
Once in a while
With a hug
A smile
A reassurance of love

A father wanting so much

To know about Afghanistan
A father wanting so much
To know about the demons
That followed my son home
A father wanting so much
To see that sparkle
In my son's eyes
Once more

I didn't think it would be like this
He and I
Islands in the same human sea
Not men sharing in his touchdown
His run-back
His high school pride
His proud performance
As he jumped into my arms
In the end zone

At bedtime
I cry
No weep
I haven't the key
To unlock
My son's misery
My son's isolation
My son's room

Damn
I didn't know
It would be
Like this

Stephanie

Never did have folks
Back home
Not much, anyway
At least not the writing kind
Got a card once
From Aunt Jessie
Said Uncle Herm – Herman
Passed away
Never really knew either
Of them

In my hands, though
Is a card
Stewart gave it to me
Stewart, a teacher
From Mississippi
He got lotsa stuff
From his kids
And he passed it out
Especially the cards

On the front
A stick figure
With a helmet
And rifle
A soldier
Kinda like me

Above in green letters
Written with a marker
"Deer Solder
"Look inside"

And I did
This is what I saw
Flowers … all sorts of flowers

Red, yellow, purple
With yellow centers
And green stems

"I don't have any money
To send you reel
Flowers
So I drew sum
For you."

It was signed
Stephanie

The card still shows
The drops
Where my tears fell
And dried

For weeks
I imagined
Stephanie was my sister
My younger sister
Who loved me so much
She would send me
A beautiful card
With a beautiful bouquet
Of flowers

I never told anyone
Except for now
Too ashamed
I guess

I carried Stephanie's card
Everywhere
And opened it

When I could
And when no one would see

Stephanie
This little girl
Who I never met
And probably never would meet

Gave me hope
And strength

And a sense
That someone else
Did care

Sorting Socks

I sat there
Sorting socks
They sat there
Watching television
And we giggled
Not at the socks
But at the cartoons

Jimmy
I called
Go check the dryer
Socks are missing
Jimmy, five,
Ran to the laundry room
Flung open the dryer door
Maaaa he screamed
No socks

As Jimmy returned
I asked
Did you eat those socks?
C'mon ... you ate our socks
He giggled
We laughed

And then Sara said
Daddy took 'em

We laughed some more

Until she scowled
And stomped her foot
He did! I saw him!
He said "I can't bring you

So I got your socks
I'll give them to the children
Who don't have any"

Jeff left two weeks ago
For a second tour
The first was rough
Real tough
He can have all the socks
He wants
I'd send him a truckload
In exchange for his safe return

Then it came to me
Socks
More socks
Our kids scurried for theirs
The ones we could give up
And I called family, friends,
co-workers
E-mailed half the world
Spread the word on Facebook
For socks
For Jeff's kids
Over there

And we stuffed boxes
Twenty of them
With socks
And trinkets
And notes
And love
And sent
Them over there

So now
When I sort socks
At night and a few
Come up missing
As they always do

I stop and think
Jeff's kids have them
God bless them
God bless Jeff

A Million Reasons

There will be
A million reasons
I don't want to talk
There will be
A million reasons
I sit staring
There will be
A million reasons
I clench my fists
There will be
A million reasons
I cry for no reason
There will be
A million reasons
I fear the night

There will be
A million reasons
I can't hug you
There will be
A million reasons
I hug you tight
There will be
A million reasons
I want to scream,
And yell, and cry
And tell you everything
All of it
All the million reasons
I can't
And won't

My Monday Letter

It is two in the morning,
No three
And I sit at the kitchen table
Where we shared bacon and eggs
And our life's worries
And joys
And I write my letter
My Monday letter
The twins sleep soundly
Boonie is asleep at my feet

It is two in the morning,
No three
And I sit at the kitchen table
And I write my letter
My Monday letter

But what to say
I haven't said before
In the Wednesday or Friday letter
And all the letters I've written
In these twelve long months

The twins - Sam and Samantha -
The best two human beings on Earth
Boonie still chases squirrels
Never catching one
And we all still laugh and laugh

And we hug tighter these days
And I sigh more
And I sleep less

It is two in the morning,
No three

And I sit at the kitchen table
And I write my letter
My Monday letter

And I look at where you sat
For breakfast
The morning you left
Boonie at your feet
The twins asking questions
Lots of questions
About planes, about GI food
About coming home
And I ask myself
About if
Not when

So I sign my letter
My Monday letter
With news about Bob and his new job
About the office staff
About my mom's operation
About my deep, deep love for you
About my prayers for you

And I promise to write on Wednesday
If not sooner

And I kiss my Monday letter
As I have done
Every letter
Ever sent
To you
My love

To Have Her Back

Just so you know
I lost my wife
Not to divorce
Not to another man
Not to boredom

No, she was killed
Over there
Way, way over there
In a place I still mispronounce
In a war I still cannot fathom
In a uniform that I thought
Would protect her
On a day when
She said peace was near
And not to worry
She'd be back
In my arms soon

I lost my wife
Her name was Allie
Her hair soft, brown, sweet-smelling
Her eyes loving, hazel, welcoming
Her frame small, straight, proud
Her voice tough, sweet, soft

We hoped to have a family
We hoped to own a house
We hoped to laugh and love
We hoped to play, sit, pray together
And let the clouds flow by overhead
And let the grass grow under our feet
And let the world swirl around us
As we made love
Passionately

And I sit
In my walled-in silence
My jail of wanting
To have her back
And so I sit
Hugging our wedding picture
Opening a bottle of her shampoo
And letting her essence
Fill my being
And weeping
And weeping

Maybe I'll join her
I think
If she cannot come to me
I'll go to her

So I sit
In the shadows

Transfixed
By indecision
Suffering
From agony

Gripped
By fear
That
This is
My life
Now
And
Ever
Will
Be

Red Birds

Red birds were nesting
In the legustra
When he came home
After his first tour
It was early April
The azaleas were in bloom
The roses looked wonderful
The yard was exploding with
Color and life
Including the red birds
He so loved to watch them dart
Into the thick green bushes
But that was ... well
So long ago

He stood on the back porch
As the red birds
Like crimson shooting stars
Against the bushy green backdrop
Flew so freely
They had returned too
From their far-off land

I missed this
He said
What I asked
This
He said
Just this
Everything there
Is so complex
So hard to see
If there ever will be
A solution
If there ever will be
A day when
They can stand

By themselves
Without us

I wrapped my arm
Around him
My son
And whispered
Dinner's almost ready
Chicken and dumplings

He sighed
Very deeply
And said
I have to go back
In two weeks

It was then I felt helpless
All those years of fixing bruises
Of gluing projects
Of scaring monsters
From under the bed
Of hugs and tears

My arm tightened
He put his around my shoulder
I love you Ma
He said
And I love you Son
As the red birds
Found their nests
For the night
And we went into the kitchen
For chicken and dumplings
Just as we did
When he was a boy
What seemed
So long ago

The Washer

The washer went
The other day
The girls painted
Little Jimmy's toes

I read your e-mail
I'm sorry you
Lost Darius
And Sam

At church
We will pray
For their
Souls

The brakes went
The other day
The girls drew
Pictures for you

I read your e-mail
I'm sorry you
Lost Terrell
And Corey

At church

We will pray
For their
Souls

I looked at
A picture of you
The other day
And kissed it
And hugged it

We know you are trying
To stay steady
To be strong
For us

But please
Dear
Be strong
For you
Not us

We will survive
With
Or without
The washer

Arnie

I couldn't stop
The towers from falling
I was only twelve

I couldn't stop
The planes from attacking
I was only twelve

I couldn't stop
The people from dying
I was only twelve

I couldn't stop
All that pain
That day
I was only twelve

I'm here now
Sitting on a rock
Eating my MRE
With my platoon
Watching the valley below

Many of us were
Only twelve
Back then
On September 11, 2001

Spec First Class Arnold
From Jersey
Is one of them
He has a son, K.C.
Only three
Arnie's Dad died
In the North Tower

We all tried
To protect
Arnie
Knowing
His Dad
Died on 9-11
A firefighter
Trying to save lives

I tried
But couldn't
Stop Arnie
From being shot
That day
In a terrible firefight

When two of us
Lost their lives

But God spared Arnie
He lived
And went home
To be with K.C.
And his wife
And mother
Those he was
Trying to protect
From another 9-11

I was shot, too
But I'm here
Wounds on the mend
Heart still torn
Trying my best
To understand
It all

For now
Knowing
We helped
Arnie
Survive
And go home
Is all we really

Need to understand

At times
Though
It seems
I'm still
Only twelve

Two Beers

Gramps and I
Went to
Stella's
The local diner

A week
After I returned
A week
After hell year
A week
After I wanted
To go back
To hell

Gramps and I
Sat across
From one another
And our eyes
Flirted with contact

Gramps
Went to Vietnam
And came back
A quiet man
A stoic man
A hurt man

A man like me

We sat there
Wiping imaginary crumbs
Off the
Plastic tablecloth

The waitress

Came and sweetly
Said the specials
Pot roast
French green beans
Pecan pie
Sweet tea

Gramps nodded
I did, too

But then
Our eyes met
His old
Mine, too

I waved to the waitress
She came
I said
No tea,
Two beers
I said

Yes, sir
She said

Keep 'em
Coming
I said

A small smile
Crept across
Gramp's face

And mine, too

Massages

I used to massage
My Dad's neck
When he returned from
Weekend drills
In the Guard

I'd slip off his boots
Oooh, a bit smelly
And work the muscles
Around his neck
He ooohed and aaahed
You got the touch, girl, he said
You got the touch

At ten, those were magical words
That I had The Touch
To soothe my Dad's aches
After a tough weekend

But he left a few weeks later
To go to Afghanistan
Somewhere, we don't know
Exactly where ... we can't know

Like other families
We were there the day
My Dad and his unit left
I hugged him so ...
Might have choked him
I decided I wouldn't cry there
No, no need for my Dad to see
Punkin' he said
I'll miss your massages

I flashed my fingers

They're right here
Ready

I tried not to engage his eyes
But I did
I melted; I swallowed hard
I clenched my teeth
But I didn't cry
No, I didn't cry

I punched him on the shoulder
And said, "Tag ... you're it.
"Got to come back now."

I'll be back he said
And you'll be it
And you'll owe
Me that massage

The convoy left the Armory
People cheered
People waved signs
People looked
So longingly at
The soldiers
As they left
As they left

And then
I fell to my knees
Well out of my father's sight
And I cried
Into my hands
And I cried
And cried

Emptying
All emotion
Into my
Hands

The very hands
That so tenderly
Gave my father

His massages

The very hands
That now wrung
With tears

As I cried
And cried

Big Brother

I stood inside the hangar
With the other families
With Mom
With Dad
And my gut
Tight as a wire

The soldiers walked
From the plane
We applauded
We sought
Our loved ones
We sought
You

And there you were
My big brother
You seemed
Much larger
Than I remembered

You seemed
Not my
Big brother
But a man

You hugged Mom
You hugged Dad
And you pulled me to you

And whispered
"I thought of you
Every day, bro'"

You punched my shoulder
Like you did
When we were kids
And I realized
My big brother
Was home

But in the days to come
I realized you really
Weren't home

As you slept next door
I heard your cries
Your nightmares
Your torment

So I'd knock on your door
And sit next to you
And listen
And listen

And learned
How to be
A big brother
To you

Answering Machine

Before Dan left
Actually the day before Dan left
He finally replaced the
Answering machine

The kids giggled as
We recorded the message
"Hey, this is Dan and Sue
... And Dan Junior ... and Maggie
Leave a message ..."

Too many "To Dos"
Were on his list
Too many undones
Before he left
Not this one, though
And we laughed as
We replayed the message
At least a half-dozen times
"It works!" he proclaimed.

"Okay, I called out
Enough!
I got the message"
And Dan laughed
Along with Dan Jr.
And Maggie
We roared over a

Silly answering machine

There is no "To Do" list
Anymore
For Dan

He did all he could
For his country
And for us

It has been nearly a year
And still his voice is so fresh
His spirit so strong
As we replay each night
"Hey, this is Dan and Sue
... And Dan Junior ... and Maggie
Leave a message ..."

And sometimes
I call from work
To hear his voice
Hoping ... a false hope
He'll pick up
But he doesn't
So I have that message
I cannot muster the courage
To replace

Commander's Wife

When I said I do
I signed on
To all he does
As commander
Of one-hundred fifty soldiers
Me, I have my twenty schoolchildren
The children misbehave,
Throw things, cry
I pat backs, break up fights, and cry
No one sees, though, my tears

I'm a commander's wife
I'm like my man
Strong and brave

Only in the most private moments
Do I let the winds of fear
Blow through my heart
And take away my breath

But I stand strong
My dear
Your loving wife
As you stand strong
For me

It is who
And what
We are

Only A Lamp

Jimmy cried that night
He broke the lamp
On the television night stand
Where we sat
Watching CNN
And home movies
And news
About the war
Your war
Our war

Tears flowed
As I grasped
Jimmy to me
And told him
It's only a lamp

It's only a lamp
I said
Only a lamp

But Dad will be angry
He said
We can hide it
Until ... Well ...
A good time to tell him

I knelt before Jimmy
And said
There's nothing in this house
We could lose
Even the lamp
And be sorry

But to lose you
And your Dad
Would make my heart ache
Forever ... and ever

It's just a lamp
Only a lamp

Ordinary Day

Just an ordinary day
Lunches, laundry
Bills and ironing
School drop-off
School pick-up
Soccer, band practices
Chicken McNuggets
A Big Mac
A salad for me
A project
About Lewis and Clarke
Baked brownies for
The sale
And ironing
At 11:15 p.m.

Avoiding CNN
Please no news
Of the war
Of casualties
Let this be
Just an ordinary day

I slip into bed
Next to your empty
Pillow
My heart, so strong
So solid all day
Melts into the night
Having lived through
Just another ordinary day

Gramps

His hands were like shovels
Broad, strong, tools
My Gramps
Wide shoulders
Scratchy beard
A laugh that
Stirred horses
Scared me a little, too.

At creekside
Gramps showed me
How to bait a line
Don't squeeze the cricket
Too tight, now Son
No Gramps
I won't

He showed me
How to cast
How to wait
And wait
And wait

We caught fish
Some bream
Some bass
A catfish or two

We caught much more

Gramps taught me how things work
How people work
Can't force a machine
It'll jam up

Gramps said
Won't be no good
Can't force a man
To be a soldier
He'll freeze up
Be a danger to hisself
And his buddies

Gramps was a soldier
A great one
In that great war
Had medals stored
In a box in the closet
Didn't flash 'em
Didn't have to

But Gramps brought
Them out
When I pleaded and pleaded
So pretty they were
Crimson strips and bronze stars
Gold and blue stripes
I touched them with reverence
And Gramps often wiped his eyes

Let's go now, he would say abruptly
Got better things to do than look
At a bunch of ribbons
In a box

So we'd fish
And we'd paint the fence
And we'd tend the tomatoes
And we'd talk and talk

He told me once of a great battle
The Battle of the Bulge
He called it
When winter's freeze
And the enemy's bullets
Killed many
Where he lost his leg
Where the Great Battle
Was fought
So bitterly

I'm here
Far from home
Far from Gramps
From the creek
From his stories

Already I've seen
Too many die

Not in great battles
But in small, deadly assaults
Men, women, children
Soldiers
My friends

Oh, how I wish to sit with Gramps
Oh, how I wish to be back at
creekside
And to cast for bream and bass
And hear him laugh
So loud trees would bend
And put my hand in his
Letting my fingers be swallowed
In his secure grip
Oh, how I wish battles would end
Oh, how I wish to be brave
Like Gramps

If Only I Had Known

Love ya, too
Bye
Silence

If only I had known
If only I had known
That would be
Our last conversation
Me, a private,
Stationed in northern Iraq
You, a corporal
In southern Iraq
Wife and husband
Separated by miles
And a different mission
But joined
By the love we
Pledged to each other only
A few months ago
As husband and wife

If only I had known
If only I had known
That would be
Our last conversation
I would have asked
An infinity's worth
Of questions
I would have
Absorbed each
And every breath

Of you
Into my soul
I would have
Touched the phone
As if to feel
Your flesh
I would have ...

But I didn't
And I can't
Go back
And whisper
To you
My love
And send
A spirit kiss
A spirit hug
A spirit smile

So part
Of me
Remains
At that phone
Clinging
To that moment
When you said
Love ya, Babe

If only I had known
If only I had known

His Letters

My son
He loved to write

As a boy, he made up stories
Of superheroes
Space travel
Adventures
And the good guys always won
In my son's world

He'd read me his stories
Waving his arms
Leaping in the air
And looking at me
Intently
For approval
As I applauded
And smiled

His letters and e-mails flowed
From Afghanistan
Six, seven each week
No superheroes
No space travel
And the good guys weren't
Always winning

I felt his optimism slipping
I felt his foundation cracking
I felt his will wavering

But I can't make it all better
With a hug and an ice cream bar
Like I did when B.J. was a boy
Reading me stories
Waving, leaping
Looking for approval

No, I can't
Be at his side
So I see him
In the photographs
On the walls
On the end tables
On my desk at work
Everywhere
And I try to be strong
For him
In this
Most
Difficult
Hour
Of his
Life

Peanut Butter

Your favorite
Peanut butter
Is in the cabinet.
Crackers, too

Your favorite
Magazine
Is on the coffee table
Waiting for you

Your favorite
Steaks

Are in the freezer
Waiting for the barbecue

Your favorite
Wife
Is in our room
Ready for you

But whatever
You wish first
We're ready
For you

The Reporter

He seemed such a nice
Young man
The reporter

He came with a
Little pad
And a pen
And, I sensed,
Awkwardness

No, Ma'am
Never served
He said

He didn't want tea
Or biscuits
He sat stiff in the chair
As Billy Boy
Our Lab
Sniffed his
Trousers

But he came
Asking
Of you
My son
So soon after
We learned
The news

I squeezed
The napkin
As I dabbed tears
And he wrote
So fast
Of your life

In his little pad
I told him you
Were silly and strong
Especially through the divorce
And you made me soup
When I had my cancer
And I pinned your Eagle badge
And waved with fear
As you drove to school
For the first time
And your touchdown
And your braces
And your smelly socks
And your affection
For Star Wars

And I talked and talked
All about you
And he wrote so swiftly
In his little pad
I became lost in
How fast I talked
And even what I said

Oh, I showed him pictures
You before the prom
With Sue Ellen
So tall, so young
So handsome

I even let him see
The pictures
You didn't want
People to see
Dancing with a broom
In my pink slippers

74

And shared those letters
And e-mails
You sent to me

He asked me to read
One or two

In his little pad
I became lost in
How fast I talked
And even what I said

Oh, he said,
Three hours after starting
I've got to get back
Got my deadline
He left with some
Photos and e-mails
He promised to return

I reached
And gave him a hug
He allowed me to give

As he said
In a small voice
I'm sorry
Mrs. Johnson

I am, too,
I said
I am, too

He walked quickly
To his car
I watched as he
Drove away
Knowing in his little pad
Was your big life

Soldier Boy

It sounds so old-fashioned now
But as I look back
On that day
I fell in love
With Soldier Boy
Everything was real
Everything was fresh
Everything was important

You came to church
In that uniform
Brilliant blue
Adorned with gold trim
Your back so straight

We'd known each other
Since, well, forever
But never understood
We were meant
To be together
Like the song
My Mom loved
So long ago
And still sings
When she talks about Dad
Her husband
My father

Soldier Boy
Oh, my little Soldier Boy
I'll be true to you
You were my first love
I will never make you blue
I'll be true to you
In the whole world

I decided then
You were my
Soldier Boy
My first love
To whom I'd be true

But I knew from Mom
A soldier is more than love
More than pledges
Of being true
It is of war
It is of lands afar
It is of fear
You might
Never return
It is of emotions
No young lady
Should experience
But I decided
So firmly then
I would be patient
Just for you
I would be faithful
Just for you
I would be strong
Just for you

You can love but one girl
Let me be that one girl
Wherever you go
My heart will follow
I love you so I'll be true to you
Take my love with you
To any port or foreign shore

And you glanced at me
During the sermon
And smiled
And winked
And I knew
Oh, I knew
My Soldier Boy
You and I
Would be
One

Darling you must feel for sure
For I'll be true to you
Soldier boy
Oh, my little soldier boy
I'll be true to you

The day I heard
Your orders came
For war
I ran to your home
To tell you
How much I love you
My Soldier Boy
And your Mom said
You left at 5 a.m.
Sorry

Sorry

The word
Like a dagger
Stabbed my heart
You left

My Soldier Boy
Without
My knowing
If you shared
Your love with me

Your Mom said
He told me this:
I hope she comes by
Mom
And if she does
Mom
Give her this

She opened her palm
A button from your uniform
Your beautiful blue
Uniform
And there you became
My Soldier Boy
And I your
Soldier Girl

And I hugged your Mom
And she hugged me
As I clasped
Your button

Darling you must feel for sure
For I'll be true to you
Soldier boy
Oh, my little soldier boy
I'll be true to you

77

The Best

The best,
My son,
Was when
We shared
Your Scout
Life

The best,
My son,
Was Tiger Cubs
With orange shirts
And shared adventures

The best,
My son,
Was Pinewood Derby
Carving cars
And those races

The best,
My son,
Was the
Summer camp
When you rescued
A fellow scout

The best,

My son,
Was the
Eagle Scout
Ceremony
When this man
Cried real tears

The best
Was when
You hugged
Me tight
Before I left
For Iraq

The best
Was when
You sent an e-mail
And said
You loved me
And that
I was
The best

The best
Is being
My son's
Father

Ginger

She was golden
Like honey
Dripping with enthusiasm
A Retriever puppy
And the kids loved her
And hugged her neck
And gave her treats
And squealed when she
Licked their faces

Ginger, they called her
Ginger, their puppy
Ginger, like ginger snaps
Ginger, their puppy

She licked our hands
And our feet
And jiggled
And wriggled
And chewed our shoes
And did all those things
A puppy is supposed to do

But we parted one Saturday morning
I had to leave my family
For the unknown

Over there

I left
The boys, my wife, and Ginger
Tom and Alex, beautiful Ann
And Ginger, who wriggled
And wiggled
And licked my face
And Tom and Alex laughed
And Ann cried

I hugged Ann tight
Kissed her sweetly

The boys looked on
With Ginger
Wagging
Her tail

Under my breath
I whispered
Take care of them
Sweet Ginger
Take care of
My family

79

Hair

Long
Yeah, long
My hair was
Long
That summer
Before Dad left
That summer I tried things
Won't tell you what
Just things
And long hair

That summer
He packed his bags
And left for Afghanistan
That summer I felt free
Of him; his rules; his glare
That summer I tried things
Won't tell you what
Just things
And long hair

I wanted so much
To look in the mirror
And know
Who I was
That summer
I let my hair
Grow out

My Dad was over there
In Afghanistan
With a platoon
Somewhere
Riding the rough terrain

And I was here
Riding through town
With my platoon
Of buddies
That summer I tried things
Won't tell you what
Just things
And long hair
But as I was brushing
My hair
One morning
CNN reported
A suicide bomber
Taking soldiers
Where Dad
Was stationed

I stopped
Frozen
Watching the television
My stomach
Twisting
My heart
Sinking

And I realized
It's not about hair
It's not about me

This sounds trite
I know
Believe me
As the son of
A soldier over there
It's the way we feel

Even though
We sometimes
Don't want
To be reminded
We care so damn
Much
We'll gladly give up
Everything

Even
Hair
As I sat
In the barber chair
Yup, all of it
I said
For my Dad

The Feast

We gathered in the hall
Of the First Presbyterian Church
Winter's wind whistling
All around
The windows
So beautifully made
A stark contrast
To us
Men in uniform
With combat boots
Emblazoned with
Name tags
And insignia
As we feasted
On our send-off meal

Son
She said
Gently holding my arm
Some turkey?
She asked
Some dressing?
Potatoes?
Oh, and punch?
And pie?

She led me
Around the feast
Explaining it all
Dish by dish
Like my Gram did
On Thanksgivings
Yes Ma'am
I said
I'll have another slice

My belly bursting

And I sat between her
And her husband
A veteran, too

Between bites of turkey
Dressing, potatoes and pie
I learned over and over
How proud they were
Of me
My soldiers
Scattered around the room
Eating turkey, dressing and pie

And I thought
Can I live up?
They expect so much
These wonderful
Pie-serving people

Can I be the man
The soldier
They see

Or am I the one
Beneath the
Uniform
Stuffed with turkey
And pie
Who trembles
In fear
Of what
Is to
Come

So Cute

She slipped
Into my lap
Still dressed
In her pink tutu
So cute
I thought

Her sweetness
Her cuteness
Enveloped me
So cute
I thought

And she slipped
Her thumb
Into her mouth
My sweetness
Of three
My sweet ballerina
In my lap
So pink
So sweet

So beautiful
She picked up
My hand
The hand
That only
A month ago
Wielded a weapon
And was at war

Her velvet touch
Against my coarse skin
Her beautiful eyes
Looking longingly at me

So we hug
Tight
She sucks
Her thumb
I sigh

So cute
So cute

Locket

I sit in my easy chair
Rocking
And watching Oprah
Not listening, though
Have the sound turned down
Something about
Botox
But I like Oprah
So I watch

In my hands
Is the locket
I open and see
Two handsome young men
Jeremy and Joseph
Look at me
Proud and in uniform

And Oprah looks at me
And I look at her
And I think she is
Feeling my pain
As I weep again
For my babies
My grand-babies
Jeremy and Joseph
Jeremy was killed in Iraq
One of those roadside bombs
He was driving his officer
And the explosion they said
Tore apart their vehicle
The officer died, too.
With my Jeremy

Joseph was shot
In Afghanistan

In a firefight
He lived a while
But died

Oh, Oprah
Can you feel my pain?
Oh, Oprah
They were nice boys
A little naughty at times
But nice boys
Jeremy had a nice voice
And played the piano
Joseph loved baseball
And fishing
And I loved them so

I hold my locket
And they look back at me
Grams
They called me
Don't worry so
Grams
We'll be back
Grams
We love you

There's no Band Aid
To mend my wounds
No sweet words
To ease my pain

So I sit here
Oprah
With you and
My locket
Hoping you'll

Say something
Nice about
My boys
Jeremy
And
Joseph

They died
But will
Live
In
My
Locket
Forever

Father and Son

A father and son
Walked by
Our compound
The other day

A warm sight
A man bonding
With his
Boy

The man rubbed
The boy's hair
The boy looked up
And smiled

I smiled, too
As my heart ached
To be home
With you

Are you all right
My son
Do you know
My son
Of my love?

Did I tell you
Sincerely enough
How much
I care?

Did I tell you
Sincerely enough

How proud I am
Of you?

They walked
Down the street
Past garbage
And debris
Yet smiling
Nonetheless

Did I tell you
Sincerely enough
How much
I want to be
The man
You want
Me to be?

Did I tell you
Sincerely enough
How I ache
Having to
Leave you?

If I didn't
I'm sorry
I promise
If I return
I'll pat your back
And walk along
The street
And smile
As you smile

Grandpa

We sit here
On the back porch
The birds - wrens and robins -
Flutter around the feeder
In the crisp autumn air
The cane chair creaks
As my grandfather rocks
I stare beyond the birds
Beyond the feeders
Beyond the fence
Beyond the trees

"I can still see them"
"I can still hear them"
Grandpa says
And I know what he means

He returned from Vietnam
When my dad was just a boy
But my dad sat with him
Those moments
On the porch
When he stared into the long horizon
When he listened to sounds
Only he heard
And feel memories
Only he felt
When he sighed heavily
And told my Dad
"War's hell, Buddy"
"War's hell"

And here Grandpa and I sit
Staring into the long horizon

I reach for his hand
And grip it

He squeezes back
And we sigh
Heavily

His son
My dad
Is over there
Somewhere
A soldier
Like his dad

And we look over
The horizon
Hoping to know
If he is safe

Grandpa grips my hand
And I understand

I can feel *them*
The soldiers
Over there
My dad
And his buddies
I can feel them
Just as I can feel
My grandpa's
Warm hand

And I have never
Loved him
My Grandpa more
Than at this moment
We stare and sit
On the porch
Sharing war
In our hearts

My Story

A reporter came the other day
Wanting my story
Actually, a soldier's wife's story
"For the anniversary of 9-11"
She said

"Oh sure," I said, "Oh, sure ... needs to
be told ..."
She sat on the couch
Between two stacks of laundry
Jimmy's and Grace's
They were at school
"Sorry," I said
"No problem," she said, opening her
note pad
"We want to tell your story."

Not much to tell ... there's laundry
As you can see
And lunches
Baths at night
Story time
Bills ... lots of bills
To the doctor
To the dentist

And going to soccer
To dance
To Grandma's
To church
Oh yeah, suppers

Subway
And Domino's

And I cry so hard at night
I shake
Can't watch the news

Jimmy's a good boy
A natural first-baseman
And Angel dances so well

I visit my husband's mom
In the home
Twice a week
Bring his dad suppers

Oh yeah, about me
Well I guess that's it
Not much
To tell
Excuse me
The washing machine
Is banging again

I run
Calling back
That's my story
As I said
Not much
To tell

Prayers

When Tim
Left for Afghanistan
The ladies at the church
Took me aside and said
Prayers
We're saying prayers
We do that for all of them
The soldiers overseas

Don't you ever get weary?
I asked

So many of them
So many soldiers
So many prayers
Does it do any good?

Alice looked surprised
And said
My grandfather died at Normandy
My brother never returned from
Vietnam
My son is in Iraq
Carla said
My husband served in Desert Storm
My son is headed to Afghanistan
In two weeks

And the ladies
Shared incredible stories
Of sadness and strength
And shared their belief
In prayers

We can't change what
Happens to them
Alice said
We can pray
That whatever happens
To them
Our prayers
Will bring them home
To us
No matter
How they are

Bruised
Battered
Drained
Hurt
Changed
Forever

Prayers
Are all
We have

The Obit

Services for
Staff Sgt. Lucien "Lucky" Williams,
Born Aug. 9, 1980
In Baton Rouge, La.,
A member of the U.S. Army
Special Forces
Who died Aug. 10, 2009,
In Afghanistan,
Will be ....

The obit went on
To tell oh, so much
About Lucky's record
His medals
His schools
His valor

He is survived by his parents
Lucien and Alice Williams
His wife Denise Williams

Survived by
The obit said
Why not...
His death torments
His death leaves devastated
His death creates the
Greatest human chasm

I cannot survive
Without Lucky
Let alone be survived
By him

And is survived by
His children
A son Luke
And a daughter Charm

So the obit says
But can they survive?
I don't think so
The obit is wrong
Luke, 12, and Charm, 8,
Cannot sleep
Because they cry
Deep into the night
Cannot eat
Because they wrench
With agony
Their dad "Lucky" is gone
The obit is wrong
We don't survive

We are frozen
In this box
Of emotions
The walls
So black
So bleak

People hug us
Bring food
Call us on the phone
Send e-mails
Write notes
Even letters
To the newspaper editor

About how terrific
"Lucky" was

We hug back
Appreciate the casseroles
Return calls
And e-mails
And be pleasant

In daytime
We seem strong

At night
We weep and hug
Each other
Fragile
Frightened
Frozen
In the box
Defined
By the
Obit

Jet Plane

My father used to sing this song
Low and under his breath
I'm leavin' on a jet plane
Don't know when I'll be back
again."

"Just give it a rest"
Mom would say
To my Dad
Still suffering
From that war
"It's over."

That is until
That evening
Before I shipped out
That evening
In my room
My mom came in
When all my bags were packed
And I was ready to go
I was standing there
Inside my door

"Mom," I said
"I can never ..."

"Shhhh..."

She embraced me

"I've watched you grow up
Through baseball, Scouts,
Through the time
We almost lost you
To cancer."

And she pulled me closer

"It was then I said
To your Dad,
'He's a gift
A precious gift
To us
And only
Us.'"

I felt her heart
Pounding
Next to mine
This woman
Of strength
And beauty

I reached
For my bag
But she stopped me

"You'll go on that
Jet plane
You'll do great things
You'll be somebody
And we'll be proud.

"But remember
You'll always
Always
Be my son
My boy

"That jet plane
Will take you away
But it will
Bring you back
To me."

92

Then I remembered
The lines to that song

Now the time has come to leave you
One more time
Let me kiss you
Then close your eyes
I'll be on my way
Dream about the days to come
When I won't have to leave alone
About the times I won't have to say,
'Oh, kiss me and smile for me
Tell me that you'll wait for me
Hold me like you'll never let me go
'Cause I'm leavin' on a jet plane."

I looked around my room.

The trophies, posters and pictures
The trinkets, the memories
 And Mom
Still hugged me
As we stepped into the hall
Closing my door
The present
Soon to be
The past

The future
Soon to be
The present

As I prepared
To leave
On a jet plane

Knights

I'm nine
I have this dream

Dragons
Try to eat me
Flames come from their
Noses
And I grab a sword
And they melt it

Then the knights come
My daddy in the lead
He turns to his men
Charge
He yells
Charge
They yell

The dragons flee

And then I see
My Daddy
Walking from the mist
He's not a knight
He's a soldier
He smiles
I smile

I go to sleep
My daddy is
A knight
And
A
Soldier

How cool
Is that

So Tall

Sergeant James Oliver
Stood outside my classroom door
Oh, my, he's so tall
I thought
And waved him in
From the toe of his boots
To the top of his cap
He was all Marine
My cousin
Back from Iraq
Here to talk
With my kids
All of six and seven years
Mouths open
Eyes bulging
At Sergeant James Oliver
My cousin

He stood so tall
In front of the children
And said with a Marine's
Authoritative voice
Stand Up

And they did
How could they not

He slipped to the floor
With legs crossed
And arms out
C'mere he said

Give a soldier
A hug

And they did
How could they not

And they asked
About his insignia
His cap
His boots
His uniform

And he showed them
His MREs
And his pack
And canteen
And he joked
About cooking soup
In his helmet
And about chewing gum
In a sandstorm
And making faces
At a camel
They laughed
And laughed
I did, too

Even sitting
He was so tall
Sergeant James Oliver
My cousin

T-Shirts

I call him
My "Ants in the Pants"
Man
My man
My strong husband

But
He's
A soldier
And
He goes
And goes
Wherever

And I
Stay home
And pray
And hope
And cry

So when
He was sent
To Afghanistan
He squeezed me tight
And grinned that
Goofy grin
And told me
He'd be all right

I thought
"My Ants in the Pants"
Man
Is off doing
What his passion is
Fighting, defending, serving
But what of me?

I'm just me
His wife

I went to work
My heart still tight
From his departure

I thought
As I walked into the office
Fourteen months
He'll be gone
Fourteen months
Can I live?
Can I survive?

And there they were
My co-workers
Screaming
"Surprise!"

With t-shirts
Emblazoned
With
An American Flag
And the words
"Come Home Charlie"

My tears
Fell
So fast
So hard

And without fail
Every employee
Every Friday
Without fail

Wore
"Come Home Charlie"

For fourteen months
Every employee
Every Friday
Without fail

In my top drawer
Is my "Come Home Charlie"
Shirt
It is faded
So many washings
So many tears
And in the evenings
I'd hug the shirt
As I sat on the sofa
Where we kissed
Where we hugged
Where we didn't ask

If you don't...
If you don't...

So, there it was
My life
My friends
My co-workers
My t-shirt

And the wish
Their wish
My wish
Did come true

Charlie
Did come home
To me
My arms
My life

The Dance

He stood in front of me
All of twelve
And held out his hand
And bowed
So gentlemanly
"Ma'am"
He asked
"May I have this dance?"

I curtseyed
Gave him my hand
And we swayed
And we swung
At my brother's wedding

That week before
I shipped out
But held my son's hand
And glided across the floor
Like Fred and Ginger
With a few glitches
Which I didn't notice
Because all eyes
Were on us
My Tommy and me

Magic was happening
That night
On the linoleum
At the Elks Lodge

Tommy wanted so much
To see his daddy again

The man who left him
And who left us
He shut out his mommy
We became cold and distant
His anger grew
My sadness expanded

Until that night
He stretched out his hand
And bowed
To accept mine

And we danced
Tommy and I
Glided across
The floor
And I whispered in his ear
"You dance so well."
I stopped short
Of saying
"Like your father."

Let our son
Be himself

Tommy kissed
Me on the cheek

And in that kiss
I felt
I found my son again
And he
His mother

Shooting Star

We created this game
The kids and I
It might seem silly
To most folks
But to us
It is how
We survive
With you there
And us here

Each night
Each clear night
We stand on the deck
Look up into the
Star-speckled sky
And holler
"We love you"

Angel always
Wants the last
"We love you"

And we pretend
The stars carry
Our voices to your ears
To your heart

One night, though,
As we raised our voices
High into the sky
A beautiful star
Shot an arc across
The horizon

And Angel and Caleb
Ooohed
And were certain
Their voices would ride
The star's back
Like a Pony Express rider
To you

And we stood there
Well after the star
Had disappeared
Hoping
You'd send a message
Back to us
On the back
Of that
Shooting
Star

If I Could Fly

"If I could fly,"
Jared said the other day.
"I'd fly to Daddy."
And so I asked him
"What would you take
On your flight?"
"I'd take a picture of you
'Cus you couldn't fit.
An' Slim Jims
An' his bowling ball
An' his Saints hat
An' me!"
He laughed at "An' me!"

His eyes, so clear, so innocent
Opened wide
As he said
"I'd bring him hugs
And lots of kisses."

A four-year-old

Can be a life-saver
I had been depressed
That day
The two-hundredth and forty-fifth day
Since you left

But Jared lifted my spirits
As he talked of lifting himself
Toward you

So I drew him to me
And gave him hugs
And lots of kisses

Be safe, my dear
We are all right

And your Saints hat
And your bowling ball
Are safe where you
Left them

The Swing

Just finished
Talking with Dad
On Skype

You look tired
I told him
Been eating right?
Getting your sleep?

I'm a nursing student now
I'm supposed to notice
Supposed to care
Especially for my Dad

Don't worry, Kid
Got it all under control

Don't worry, Kid
He told me
As we swung
On the backyard swing
The day he left
For Afghanistan
The day of my
Endless tears

The day
I thought
My heart
Would
Break
In pieces
A million
Pieces

I'm a nursing student now
I'm supposed to notice

Supposed to care
Especially for my Dad

I gulped a half cup
Of strong coffee
Ate half a muffin
Hoisted my heavy
Pack
On my bony shoulders
Over my scrubs
Fumbled for my keys

Just before I plowed
Out the door
I noticed
The breeze
Had rocked
The swing
In the backyard

And it caught
My eye
I sighed
And whispered
What the ...

I dumped my pack
And keys
And darted
Out the door to
The swing

How long had it been
Oh, so many years
Higher, Daddy
Higher, Daddy
I'd yell with glee

Hold tight
He'd say
And laugh
With me
As I laughed, too

That morning
I sat and
Pushed myself

The old ropes creaked

My heart sank

I whispered
Into the air
Daddy, please be safe
Daddy, please come home
I need you
To push me
Higher
And
Higher

Sons

My sons
So different
Yet so much the same
One a roughneck
Charging through life
Home runs, touchdowns
Cheers, waves to the crowd
Waves to me in the stands
Hunting and fishing
And disarming me
With his smile

The other
Bold
But careful
Studious
And generous to a fault
Loved to build
And create
And disarm me
With his smile

War came
They sacrificed
Dark wavy hair
For high-tight
Their freedom
For regimentation
Their disarming smiles
For stern salutes
And swapped fishing poles
And hammers
For rifles

My sons
So different
Yet so much the same
One a sniper
The other an airman

Am I proud?
Oh, yes I am

I'm also terrified
Of the phone call
Or the knock
That would drain
My heart and soul

So I go to work
Watch silly shows on television
Read romance novels
Call friends
And never let a second
Pass
Without thinking
Of my sons
So different
Yet so much the same

Offering
Their hearts
Their souls
Their lives
For me
For
Our
Country

The Airplane

I was five
Maybe six
Daddy took me to
King's Department Store
Where I spotted the
Most wonderful thing
A balsa wood airplane
In a plastic bag
Assembly required of course

And we bought the treasure
For one dollar and twenty-nine cents
And carefully assembled the wings,
The tail, the wheels
And the all-important
Nose stabilizer ... actually a chunk
Of metal that slipped over the
Balsa plane's nose

And I ran to the street
Glee doesn't do justice
To my anticipation
And daddy pulled his arm back
With the airplane in his fingers
And there it went
Gliding effortlessly
Over Mrs. O'Byrne's bushes
And over Mr. Dylan's truck
Airborne ... on a mission
An important mission

And Daddy and I ran
Our arms waving
At the airplane
The balsa airplane
The one in a plastic bag

On a hook at
King's Department Store
Only that morning
Now airborne
On our street
So beautiful

And the airplane glided
So silently
So carefully
To a spot on our street
Where it landed
And waited for us
As any airplane would
That had accomplished
Its mission

I picked up the airplane
Daddy rubbed my hair
And said
That's a good plane, Son
I looked up at Daddy
And grinned
Holding the airplane
In my arms
And said
The best
Airplane
Ever

We had supper that night
Spaghetti and meatballs
And lots of bread
Didn't eat much salad

That night

Daddy took me into his arms
And told me what I kinda expected
He told me he would have to go back
To that place called Iraq
That he'd be leaving soon
That they needed pilots
To fly their airplanes

I was five
Maybe six
But I understood
Our airplane
Was his way of trying to prepare me

For what was to come
We sat on my bed
The airplane in my lap
His arm around me
Daddy trying to be brave
Me trying to be brave
And so
We sat
Together
With
The airplane
The best airplane
Ever

Alicia

My words
Powdery soft
I am lilac essence
I am gentle
Embraces
I am sweet
Whispers

I am not
All those
Things
You endured
You braved
You saw
Those
Things
That threatened
To strip
Goodness from
Your heart
And soul

I am none
Of those things
I am your
Alicia
I am yours

Darkness

May have followed you
But I will fight
To reclaim
The man
I knew

I will bear
Your load
I will envelope
Your fears
And extinguish
Them
With the
Fires of love
I will not stop
I will not fear
I will not surrender

I will bring you home
Second by second
Minute by minute
Hour by hour
Day by day
Year by year
Until your torment
Silently slips
Into the
Distant
Past

Seared

That day
That hour
That minute
Was seared
Into my memory
My life

The American Flag
Snapped
In the wind
Outside the Armory
Mom pulled her
Red, white and blue
Flannel coat around her
As my Dad
Slung his duffel bag
Over his shoulder

He and I finished the fort
That summer
And went fishing
Lots of times
Caught bass and bream
And other fish
And laughed
And hugged
We painted the house
That summer
The mint green
Mom wanted
And we endured

We saw the race cars
We listened to the hoot owls
We became us
Like we never
Had been

That summer
Father and son
Dad and me

He wrapped his arm
Around my shoulders
One night
One sticky Southern night
One beautiful sunset night
One I-love-my-Dad night

You're the best Son
You know
He said

You're the best Dad
I said

So we sat
The best
Son
The best
Dad

Cicadas sang
Loblolly pines
Swayed
Crickets
Chirped
And the wind
The warm wind of summer
Swirled and touched
Our cheeks
On the back porch
Me with my Dad
The best Dad

And here we are
He's going
To war
With the Flag
Snapping
With my arms wanting
To keep him here

But I know
He needs to
Go over there

So I stand on the tarmac
Trying to savor
This moment
This wonderful moment
Seared in our memory

And here we are
My Mom and me
Waving
At the blue bus
Waving
As if our arms
Could send a cloak
Of safety
To him
As if our arms

Could ease
The fear
That is seared
In our hearts
Our eyes

As my Dad
Goes
Over there
And we stay here

I wish I weren't
A kid
So I could go with
My Dad

But I can't
So I'm here
His son
Seared
By his love

Seared
By my desire
To hug
Him again
And again

Shrine

The other night
I sat
On our couch
Ginger
Lay near
My feet
And I looked
At all your photos
And your certificates
And wondered
Should I take them down
Box them up

Let your memory
Exist only in my heart
And not on the walls
And shelves

The other night
At night
I sat
On our couch
Ginger
Lay near
My feet

Tears slid
Down my cheeks

Again
As I curled
On the couch
And decided
I'm not ready

You were the best
The bravest
The most
Of anything
I ever wished for
So here I sit
Not caring
If it's a shrine
To you

I know
This is the best
And only
Way
To keep you
In my
Life
As long
As my heart
Continues
To yearn
For you

Mom's Eyes

What was it
About Mom's eyes
That made me crumble?
That made me
A Marine
A man
A skilled soldier
Crumble
Like a child
A boy
Of three
What was it?

My crisp uniform
I wore so proudly
That morning
At graduation
At Camp Lejeune
The flags, the music, the pride
Of the Marine Corps
Worn on my sleeve
Embellished in my heart
Engraved in my soul
A Marine

And I saw mom's eyes
So soft
So gentle
Like they were
When she baked brownies
In the kitchen so far back home
Like they were
When she patched
My skinned knee
When she
Watched my school play

When she
Cheered my team
When she ...

I stand tall
My chin strap is tight
My mind is focused
My heart pounds
At my Marine
Graduation

I glance and see
My mom's eyes
So pretty
So proud
She smiles
I feel
So strong
So warm
So loved

That day
Was the best
The proudest day
Of my life

The day
This Marine
On the outside
Stood straight
Like a soldier

But inside
Melted
Like
A child

The Cross

I mended her
Torn skirts
And made her
Matching clothes
With her dolls

She'd giggle at
Pillows with Happy Faces

My girl brought me joy
And pride....

Especially when she
Marched to graduation
At Basic
Holding the Guidon
Ahead of her squadron

I swallowed that pride
And my tears when she told
Me of her orders
To Afghanistan
No pattern was created
To stitch a smile
On my worried face

That morning
She left
I slipped into her
Hand a cross
I sewed the night before
"Thanks, Momma."
"I love you."

I gave her one more thing
A kiss on her cheek

Like I did when she was little
That was fourteen months ago
And she is back now
Her eyes etched with sights
And sounds only she knows
Her face stitched
With threads
Of trials
I can only imagine

We sit on the couch
Where we sewed together
And laughed and embraced
And ate popcorn
And watched silly moves
And told secrets
And sampled cheap cologne
And painted nails
And cried
At sad movies
And became best friends again

This night
No laughter
No secrets
Just tears
As she sits silent
And slipped from her pocket
That cross
And gripped it
And she held my hand
And I tried so hard
To feel through her fingers
What she couldn't say
With her words

Passing the Time

They said don't watch CNN
They said keep busy
Church work
Sewing circle
Bridge club
School volunteer
They said
It will be better
Passing the time

But nothing works
No magazine
No hook rug
No garden
No card game
Blots you
From my mind
From my heart
From my soul

Inside I scream
For you
No one sees
My agony
Though
I've become good
At passing the time
In a way no one sees
How brittle
I've become

Little Hand

I touched
His little hand,
My son
Born premature
Born there

I'm here
Touching his little hand
On the screen
My love smiles
Childbirth exhausting her
War exhausting me

I breathe in their love
It infuses me with energy
His little hand
Her loving eyes
From so far away
I touch the screen
Wishing so much
I could electronically
Slide into it

And into her arms
And kiss her
And him
And give them my strength

Damn
The screen goes blank
Sirens blare overhead

And it happens again
We go into the danger
Swallowing hard
Gritting teeth
Sighing heavily

Me, I pray hard
I'll be back

To my screen
To her eyes
To his
Little hand

My Flag

Wind whipped the flag
Over our headquarters
That morning
My platoon and I
Shipped out
To Afghanistan

My heart filled
With pride
As the flag snapped
And twirled above us
As we
In our vehicles
Waved to
Family lining
The road

But the most special flag
Wasn't on a pole
No, it was
In my arms

That flag
Was paper and crayon
And wonderful

Drawn the night
Before
By my little sweetheart
The best girl in the world
She wrote
"American soldiers are the best"

I'm a big guy
Yet I choked up
As we rolled away
And I saw my princess

Blowing me a kiss
And I pressed
On my window
Her flag of paper
And crayon

Tears rolled down my cheeks
She didn't see, though
Only my big arm
Out the window
Waving and
Waving
Hiding my emotions

She didn't hear
Me whisper
I love you, Angel

As the tires rumbled
Through the streets
Lined by wonderful
People
Flag-holders
Veterans
Children with
Flags of their own

And yet, my most
Precious flag
Was in my arms
From my angel

My flag of paper
And crayon
My flag
Of wonderful

Sunset

I never paid much attention
To the sunsets
Until you told me
Of the sunsets
Over the Euphrates
How the yellows turned
To golds
And the reds
To crimsons
And the sky
Bathing everything
In a golden hue

So each night
At sunset
I stand at the back porch
And watch
Nature's show

And hope
You are standing
Over in Iraq
Admiring your
Sunset
As I admire
Mine

On Alert

Been to Afghanistan
Seen and heard
Felt and smelled
Too much
Too much

Came home
Sweetness
Love
Kisses

Mowed the lawn
Ate at Dairy Queen
Snuggled in our bed
Played with Jimmy and Angel
In the pool
As the sun warmed us
Watched Toy Story I, II and III
Over and over
Laughed and laughed
Oh, how we laughed
Burned the popcorn
We laughed so much

On orders now
On alert now

To return
And I hear the sounds again
And see the scenes again
Bombs, smoke, chaos

And, if you can understand,
I want to return
To leave my honey
Jimmy, Angel

And go

My buddies do, too

I can't explain
Maybe the sweetness of my home
The beauty of my love
And our children
Tells me
They'll be all right

As I leave
To rejoin
The soldiers
Who help the helpless

Start Again

It went badly that night
I deployed

Inside I was hurting,
But outside I hurt you.

Oh, how I pray
We can start again.

I don't know, dear
What ran through my mind.

Hurt you and I'll feel better
About leaving you behind.

Oh, how I pray
We can start again.

Silky hair, jasmine cheeks,

Soft skin, tender kisses.

Oh, how I pray
We can start again.

I can't doubt myself here,
Lest I risk my men.

I can't doubt myself here,
I'll go insane.

But oh, how I pray
We can start again.

Your voice so sweet;
Your gaze so passionate.

I'm sorry I hurt you;
Can we start again?

The Letter

Two weeks
After they came
To tell me of your death
Two weeks
After I crumbled and cried
Came your letter, my son,
My dear son,
A beautiful, strong boy

I opened your letter
I immediately began
To cry
Even before I knew
What you said

I'm walking down
The streets of Fallujah
It's going okay
So far
People seem nice
It's all so strange
I want to be home

Tomorrow
We head to
The market
And meet
The people
We're here
To protect
I'm so excited
I feel I'm
In the right place
At the right time

The letter didn't tell
Of the bomb

Of the explosion
Of the end
Of my son

And so I sit
At the dinner table
Your father
Your brother
Your sister
And we cry
And we pray

And they ask
To hear once more
The letter
Your letter
The letter
You wrote in the
Final days
Of your life

I can't read the letter
Out loud
It hurts too much
I miss you so much
So I carry your letter
With me everywhere
The market
The choir practice
The dinner table

Each day
Each moment
I touch your letter
It is as if
I were touching
You

My Daddy

A second grade teacher asked her students to write a paragraph: "My Daddy." This is one of them, with some poetic license.

MY DADDY
My Daddy has big hands
They are Daddy's Hands
He lifts me with One Hand
My Sister with the Other Hand
We giggle and Yell
Put us Down
My Daddy eats a hamburger
In one hand
And Corn on the Cob
In the other

My Daddy is Big
I am Little
My Daddy is fuzzy

I am soft
My Daddy is in a place
I can't spell
He is not Here
With Me
And my Little Sister

He is Brave
And Tall
And Wears
Big Boots
And a Rifle

My sister cries
Cuz Daddy is there
So I hug her
Like Daddy did

Sometimes
I cry, too

The Hour

I sit at my bunk
At the hour
We told
Each other
We'd hold
Dear
Sacred

I imagine you
Sitting
On our bed
Tired
Exhausted
Wondering
If I'm with
You too

I sit here
On our bed
Tired
Exhausted
Knowing
I'm with you
As I promised
This minute
This hour

And then
I breathe in
The cologne
You always wore
And then
I recreate
Your words
Be safe

I'll be here for you
Be safe

And so
I sit here
Tired, exhausted
And invite
You
To invade
This minute
This hour

And from that
Hour
And from that
Minute
I absorb your strength
Across all these miles
And all these days
And I feel
The wonder
As if
We are
Meeting
Again
For the
First time

It is at these
Moments
I know
I love you
I always
Will

Holding On

The girls are asleep
Cat in the Hat
Helped them drift off
They miss stories
From Daddy's mouth

I miss the smell
Of your work shirts;
The feel
Of your strong hands

I sigh
It's two in the morning
And I'm
So alone

I keep holding on
Staying strong

At church today,
Friends said
They'd pray for us
I smiled and nodded
And thanked them
And hugged them

I keep holding on
But so alone
I miss you asleep
Next to me
I miss making
Your coffee
In the morning
I miss it all

I keep holding on

My Dad

It's November 21
My dad's birthday
He is
Well, sixty-something

I don't have
A cake, Dad
No candle
No gift

I'm here though
In this war.
Like you were
In yours

I feel now
What you felt
And what you kept
Locked in your soul

I know now
What you knew
And what
You couldn't tell me

I know now
Like you

I'll never
Be the same.

Sometimes
I feel
Sixty-something
Too

If only
I could feel
Your broad arms
Around my shoulders

If only
I could hear
You say again
I love you.

If only
I could sit
In your awesome
Presence

I know now
Why I should
Have loved
You more

The Hard Times

They come too frequently
The hard times
Too much month
At the end of the paycheck
Too many bills
Too many days
I wish you were back with me
Too many times I cheer
For Jimmy to get a hit
And he looks back at me
And I can see in his eyes
He wishes you were here
Too many times Angel
Dances like a beautiful ballerina
And peers into the audience
For me ... and you
They know, my dear,
You are over there

The hard times
You live through
Must be agony
Compared to ours
My dear

So we give
Double hugs
And extra kisses

And say a prayer for you
And your buddies
We get water from the bathroom
sink
'Cause it tastes better
And leave the hallway light on
And make sure the doors are
locked
And the dogs have water
The way Daddy did

And I slip into our bed
And sigh from weariness
From the hard times
Of today
Knowing mine are
Nothing
Compared to yours

As darkness
Surrounds me
I pull your pillow
Close
And try to feel
Your strength
And send
You
Mine

Dad

Every step
My son took
I greeted with enthusiasm
Yeah, I was one of those dads

Cheered
As he swung at the baseball
Swatted at the puck
Shot the basketball
Yeah, I cheered
And often
Too loud
And felt
So lucky
To be his Dad

We made kites
Went to the zoo
Went camping
And cooked stuff
Under the stars
With noises all around

And I felt
So lucky
To be his Dad

That moment
Though

On the flight line
Just before his unit
Shipped out
I felt weak
Crippled inside
But never let it show

Because
I felt lucky
So lucky
To be his Dad

He walked straight
And strong
To the plane
I wanted so much to run
And grip him
Whisper selfishly
In his ear
Come home Son
I don't think
You're ready yet

But I didn't
I stood proud
With the other dads
Beaming with pride
But aching with fear

Daddy Now?

The wind whistled through
The willows
Their gentle, green arms
Draped in an earthly embrace

At Oak Grove Cemetery
At 11:18 in the morning
The willows filtering the sun
But not my agony

Before me was the casket
With Private First Class
Jacob Andrew Robinson
My son

Cherry wood gleamed in the sun
As I sat so solemn
Trying not to weep
Not for me but for the
Little man who sat next to me
Jacob Andrew Robinson Junior
Who held my hand so tight
Whose hand I held so tight
His momma died at childbirth
And now his dad died
Being so brave

"Taps" played
And I forced back tears

So crisp was the sergeant
In his uniform
As he handed me

The flag so firmly folded
Into a triangle

I embraced the flag
And Jacob Andrew Robinson Junior
Put his hand on the stars
A boy of three
How could he understand?
How could I help him understand?

The ceremony was over
We walked hand in hand
Back to the car
The big black car
With American flags
The sound of "Taps"
Still ringing in my ears

We slipped into the back seat
He sat tight next to me
I put my arm
Around his small shoulders
And rubbed his hair
And pulled him close to me

He looked up
His pretty blue eyes
Like gems
The same eyes
His father had
And he asked
Are you my Daddy now?

Dear Sue

I hold your letter
In my lap
Every night
Sometimes I fall asleep with it
And two o'clock comes
The television is still on with CNN
The night is still young
And once again I long for you

There is your letter
The first you wrote to me

I'm not much for writing

You said in black ink on white lined
paper

Never written a letter like this before
Never wanted to ... 'til now
Dear Sue

It's hard to tell you
What it's like
Tight, it squeezes tight
It's hard to breathe sometimes
With the tension
I stay alive
For you
I'm sorry
Not much of a letter writer
Love
Mike

And I bring the letter
As I have done each night
Into our room
And lay it on your pillow
As I wrestle to sleep
Next to ... you

Those Arms

I love the way your arms
Surround me
Strong
Sure
Manly

Those arms
Brought me to you
A wonderful night
Years ago

I was eager
And fulfilled
And engaged
In your love
My most
Wonderful man

Can't wait
To let you
Wrap those arms
Around me
Again

Brother

My brother
The football star
The soccer star
The school star

I knew enough
At school
To slide
Into the background
Of my brother
The football star
The soccer star
The school star
The North star
Of my life

That morning
At breakfast
He stood
I knew what
He was to say
He told me
The night before

Mom, Dad
I've enlisted in
The Marines

Wow!
What a man
I thought
Me, at fourteen
Him at nineteen
The football star
The soccer star
The school star
The North star

Of my life

"Marines" rolled off my tongue
Like a prayer
That my brother
Jim would be
A peacemaker
Be the star
I never could
Or would be
Afflicted
As I am
In this
My
Chair

That night
He knelt
Before me
I'm scared
He said
I'm scared

I said
Buddy,
I'm scared, too

So that night
A dark night
Sliced by slivers
Of stars
He said
To me
You've been brave
All these years
In school fighting
Your way

Through the halls
Fighting those looks
Fighting those attitudes

When it seemed so easy
For me
You've been my inspiration
I've never told you this before
Brother

I sat speechless
Jim ... said ... I ... was ...
His ... inspiration
We sat silent for a while
Until I punched him
In the shoulder

Hey, he asked
What was that for?
And I smiled
He knew then
I loved him
Without saying it
And he loved me
Without saying it

We're brothers
The best damn

Brothers

The next day
He left
He looked so sharp
So dedicated
So Marine
When he turned my way
With a salute

I crumpled
In my chair
I couldn't salute back
So I forced back
Tears ...
I didn't cry ...
I wouldn't cry ...
Not until
That night
In my room

When I acknowledged
My brother
Was gone
And I felt
So alone

Finding Myself

Iraq?
Mom asked as I stuffed
Myself with her pancakes

Yes, Mom
Iraq
I'm going to Iraq
Yes, Mom
I volunteered

Silence ... a long silence
The only sounds were of
Food being prepared
And eaten
And heavy sighs

I'm a Marine now, Mom
It's what we do

But deep in my soul
I knew I really wanted
To find myself

And I was convinced
The fires of combat
The threat of fear
The test of comradeship
Would be where I would
Become a man
Unlike my father
Who left us
Unlike my uncle
Who drank too much
Unlike my brother
In jail

The family honor
Was placed squarely
On my shoulders
Not just to find myself
But to define who
I am

Yes, Mom
Iraq

Our Son

What a wonderful
Brave son we have

It was bedtime
After bath
After toothpaste
After hair brush
He and I knelt
At his bedside

"Dear Lord,"
We prayed
"Keep Daddy safe
Each and every moment
Amen"

Curtiss added a new prayer

That night on our knees
"Give Momma strength
So when Daddy comes back
She can hug him tight."

I swallowed
And hugged Curtiss
And rubbed his hair
And whispered
"I love you."

He grinned and said,
"I know ... love you, too."
He slipped into bed
With a grin on his face
A tear on mine.

I'll Return

The sky turned angry
The wind smelled of hate
As thick clouds swirled
Our way
That day I tried to write
A letter to you
When wind-whipped
Sands
When angry skies
Darkened
When I felt hell
Around me
That day
I wanted to tell you
How much I love you
And that I'll return
To you arms

I choked
Like never before
With the thickness
Trying to breathe
Trying to live

When I felt hell
Around me
That day
I wanted to tell you
How much I love you
And that I'll return
To you arms

Mortars
IEDs

Bullets
Traps
Fighting
Those who
Sent death
Our way

All these months
I've been strong
All these months
I've kept the hope alive
That you and I would
Be enveloped
In each other's arms
And that I'll return
And the power of your love
Will renew my life

But I'm here
Each day draining
My spirit
My soul
My strength
My life

The only hope
I have
Is that I'll return
Again
To you

My love
My dear
My life

If I Told You

If I told you
The truth
You would not
Be able
To be strong
For Caleb and Cassie

If I told you
How I feel
You would not
Be able
To be strong
For you and for me

If I told you
Everything
It would grip
You too much
As it does
Me

So I tell you
It's okay
I'll be home soon
So I tell you
It's okay

But it's not.
Our hearts

Thump with fear
Our eyes
Keep watchful
Our days
And nights
Are sliced
Minute by minute
Sound by sound
Sigh by sigh

So I tell you
It's okay
I'll be home soon
So I tell you
It's okay

If I told you
The truth
That same
Fear I feel
Would move
Into our house
And then
I couldn't
Live
With
Myself.

Our Lives

I live in Indiana
My sister lives in Iowa
She asked, "How do you do it?
How do you live without him?"

You see
I'm not a brave person
Married
To a soldier, a warrior, among
The few, the proud, the brave

He sends me letters
Actually only cards
They lay on my bed
Brief, beautiful passages of
Love and faithfulness

I decided when he left
I could not drain his strength
The strength I knew he needed

Our lives, then
Are intertwined
With love, with understanding
With thoughts
He'll be in my arms again,
And I'll be in his

Until then, I fight the urge
To sound afraid
Even though I am
To sound alone
Even though I am
To sound anxious
Even though I am

You see,
My strength
Lies
In knowing
He has his

Reality

Reality?
Welcome to mine
Not the Jerry Springer reality
That's not it
Reality is not hearing
From him
For four days
Afraid
The silence
Is deadly

Welcome to reality
Not the Martha Stewart reality
That's not it
Reality is asking my neighbor
To borrow a couple of diapers
And, please, a cigarette
Maybe two

Welcome to reality
Not the daytime soaps
That's not it
Reality is the drive-through
Reality is overdrawn checks
Reality is the Salvation Army
Thrift Store
Reality is the notice that
The power will be turned off
Reality is Spaghetti-Os
Reality is medicine for
Our daughter and not for me
Reality is seeing the flag
Fly outside our home
And remaining proud
Reality is hurting so much
Reality is going to bed
Without his hugs

Reality is waking up
And starting reality
All over again
And again
And again

They've got it all wrong
The television people
The politicians
The commentators
The ones who don't
Have a clue
About my reality

My son, Seth, is seven
My daughter, Angie, is five
And we have a boy
On the way
They're sweet kids
Kiss their dad's picture
Each and every night
That's our reality
They clean their rooms
They help Mom
That's our reality
They don't complain
They hug me so tight
That's our reality
They love unconditionally
They don't realize
What reality really is

It's praying you'll be home
It's hoping for a better life
It's fearing the worst
It's being strong
On the outside

Suffering from weakness
On the inside
That's my reality
Each hour
Each day
Each week
Each month

And I keep
My reality
From you

You have so much
To fear
To worry about
In your life

On the edge
Of a razor

Your reality
Is so much
More
Deep
Dark
Fearful
Than
Ours
My
Love

Be
Safe

About the Author

G. Mark LaFrancis has been a writer for more than twenty-five years, mostly in journalism. He has won many local, state and national writing awards as a reporter and columnist. He is a retiree of the Armed Forces, which he served for twenty-three years in the Air Force, Air National Guard and Air Force Reserve. During his years of service, he earned two Air Force Commendation Medals.

He is employed at the local community college where he manages public relations and marketing, teaches journalism and broadcasting, and advises the award-winning campus newspaper.

He has been a Boy Scout leader, a youth group leader, and mentor to young writers.

"Without the good Lord guiding me, I could not be a success at anything. I thank God for my family, my community and my talents."

For More Information:
Web site: www.inspiringauthor.org
Facebook: In Their Boots: Poems Inspired by Soldiers and Their Loved Ones

M&M Book Publishing Co
9 Janice Circle
Natchez, MS 39120
gmarklafrancis@hotmail.com

Our Soldiers
And Loved Ones:
Pray for
Them

www.ingramcontent.com/pod-product-compliance
Lightning Source LLC
Chambersburg PA
CBHW072023040426
42447CB00009B/1702